C0-BJH-156

DEPARTURE FROM INDIFFERENCE

DEPARTURE FROM
INDIFFERENCE

PROBING THE FRAMEWORK OF REALITY

OCTAVIO A. MELO

Copyright © 2019 Octavio A. Melo
Published by Fallen Leaf Publishing

All rights reserved. No part of this publication may be reproduced, stored in a retrieval system or transmitted, in any form, or by any means, electronic, mechanical, recorded, photocopied, or otherwise, without the prior written permission of both the copyright owner and the above publisher of this book, except by a reviewer who may quote brief passages in a review.

The scanning, uploading, and distribution of this book via the Internet or via any other means without the permission of the publisher is illegal and punishable by law. Please purchase only authorized electronic editions and do not participate in or encourage electronic piracy of copyrightable materials. Your support of the author's rights is appreciated.

Interior design by Vince Pannullo
Printed in the United States of America by
BooksJustBooks.com

ISBN: 978-0-9838047-2-7

CONTENTS

PREFACE

On the popular T.V. show *Star Trek: The Next Generation,* a common refrain heard from Commander Data (an android) is that he would like to be able to feel. This represents a familiar theme in science fiction, with machines wanting to reach a state where they are capable of some sort of emotions or feelings. But what does it mean to "want" anything? It means that the entity that is doing the wanting is, in reality, experiencing some sort of *yearnings* or *desires,* which are feelings themselves. Therefore, when Data states that he wants to be able to feel, he is, in effect, expressing a feeling—and this, if taken at face value, means he is already in a state of both being able to experience feelings and of acting on them. The error here is that the point being presented is analyzed independently from the agent who is making (and providing evidence for) the point in question—the two are inexorably mixed. This lapse in logic is forgivable in a show with the objective of providing some form of mass entertainment, but more serious works and treatises, especially those that explore the nature of reality, must be held to a higher standard.

In a general sense, how most individuals view life is that we are responsible for our actions and should strive to do some measure of good, and there is a vague sense that what we do, or fail to do, somehow has a larger meaning. We also have a sense of right and wrong (sense of value), which is deeply ingrained into our beings, with this sense being a presence in all our endeavors, including our attempts at understanding different aspects of reality (agreeing or disagreeing with anything, including this point, is an example of using this sense of value).

But as we go through life, we deal with difficulties and challenges, the significance of which is not always clear. This tests our understanding of what is right, loosens whatever grip we have on our convictions, and leads us to question whether or not our values are worth holding on to. Religions and spiritual traditions provide forums that address these questions, and they make their cases as to why theirs is the better way. At the opposite end, there are groups that posit that we are basically just matter and that everything is explainable in an empirical sense with there being no larger meaning, and they too make their cases as to why theirs is the better approach to life. Even though these different views have our sense of value as a common undercurrent, the results are often confusing and contradictory, with one group stating that what has value is the exact opposite of a different group's position—more seldomly discussed is the source and significance of this sense of value.

But for any position or view to be considered valid, it must rest on the principles of reason and logic. And this process of determining the validity of a position must begin with identifying the underlying premise—along with its limitations—and then ensuring that it works from within these limitations. For example, if you were to ask an individual if she speaks English and she responds, "No, I wish I did, but never had an opportunity to learn" you would clearly see that the response is not logical. And the stronger the case that this individual makes as to why she would like to learn English, the weaker the original premise becomes. For instance, if she continues in English, referring to the prominent position of the United States in the arena of world affairs and how English is becoming the language of technology and so forth, you might be taken in by the eloquence of the delivery or by the logic of the points themselves, but you must not lose sight of the fact that, like

Data, she is making use of a tool (in her case, the ability to speak English) that does not exist in her defined arsenal. A hard line must be drawn around the limitations set by the premise, and it must be observed rigorously, otherwise the position becomes invalid.

Of the views that are prevalent today, many suffer from a similar shortcoming where the position is analyzed, sometimes brilliantly, but the arguments themselves stray beyond the limitations set by the premise. This work attempts to avoid this trap and also to sidestep some of the confusing rhetoric by focusing directly on the foundations for our understanding of reality and on their inherent limitations. It is a reasoned substantiation of the notion that some things do indeed matter—and why. No positions are presented here that require specialized learning or that use a "that's just the way it is" type of reasoning. The methods used to arrive at any conclusions are based on the principles of reason and logic—the steps are outlined, and the arguments are open to and inviting of the highest level of scrutiny.

The questions in this work were selected because of the roles they play in our views of life. They are, for the most part, in some form or another, of great significance to anyone who ever wondered whether there is meaning and purpose to it all. Because our understanding of life and what has value contributes heavily to the direction we give our actions, it becomes ever more important that this understanding rest on sound logical principles. This work is an attempt to explore these themes, with the only requirements being a willingness to reflect on these matters and an openness to venturing beyond the boundaries set by convention.

PARTICLES

Matter exists. We can use this as a starting point—that the material world exists, along with its qualities and characteristics (time, space, energy, gravity, particles, and so forth). Even though there are questions about the description of these elements, there is very little contention that we live in a material world. A deeper question, one that is often heard in differing forms, is if there is anything beyond matter.

There are many ways to go about tackling this question, but a logical starting point would be to try to determine if everything can be explained in a material sense or if there is anything that falls outside of a material explanation. Putting aside questions of dark matter/dark energy that account for most of what makes up the known universe (because so little is known about them), the basics are that atoms are the building blocks of matter, and the universe has been expanding since the big bang approximately 13.8 billion years ago. And all the activity in the universe is governed by fundamental physical forces and subjected to material characteristics and laws. For instance, within vast interstellar clouds in space, gravity helps to attract (mostly hydrogen) atoms together, creating a concentration where pressure and temperature gradually increase until conditions reach such an extreme that there is nuclear fusion, which in turn leads to the formation of other elements. This, in a most general sense, is how stars are formed and function, a process that takes millions and billions of years.

For the most part, most material processes can be explained in a similar manner: by adding, replacing, or rearranging particles, or by exposing particles to certain conditions, certain changes and outcomes can consistently be expected. We can use this approach to explain why planets orbit stars, why weather patterns are the way they are, why water expands when it freezes, or even how artificial intelligence works (binary code), and so forth, behind these and any other activity, is a material principle or law driving it. Because these principles or laws cannot be broken, we can make the case that in a universe of particles bouncing around, no two particles ever "bumped" into each other the wrong way.

Within this same vein, when it comes to giving an account of humanity, no matter what our views may be or how strongly we feel about certain positions, the underlying fact is that, materially speaking, we are nothing but mere arrangements of atoms—vast, intricate, and complex arrangements of atoms—but just atoms nonetheless. We are therefore bound, within this context, to using only the properties of these units of matter when providing an explanation for human characteristics—and nothing more. But this is where the "matter only" explanation of the universe comes up short.

Even though we are material beings—collections of atoms in a vast universe where there are no "wrongs"—we have a sense of right and wrong, along with an ability to experience, and act on, a plethora of other sensations that cannot be described strictly in material terms. The universe itself, which is shot through with majestic splendor and savage beauty, which boggles the imagination with its immensity and beckons humanity with the prospect of conquering untold frontiers, has as one of its most defining features a sheer indifference—it may stir profound feelings in those who observe it, but the universe knows nothing of these things. It does not rejoice as it blithely expands into the indescribable, nor does it despair at the fate that awaits it once its cycles are spent—the universe simply does not, and cannot, care. But we care, and no physical process describes how atoms are able to develop the ability to care, or to feel, or to reach a state of awareness…. And it should be pointed out that at this stage of the argument what we actually feel about this position is completely irrelevant—what is of significance is that we have the ability to feel, to care, to experience reality, and to wonder about these questions—and this sense of wonder, which cannot be anchored in matter, must not be excluded from our observations.[1]

Therefore, because matter is unable to escape the grasp of indifference and feelings at any level represent a distinct departure from indifference, then any indication of a sentiment or of a feeling

---

[1]The question here is whether there is an atom (or even subatomic particle) in the human body that has the ability to experience any sensations. And any response to this question that is not an unqualified "no" goes directly against all our understanding of the characteristics of matter. The problem, then, for a materialistic premise is that once atoms and particles are eliminated from consideration, there is nothing left to consider in our attempts to identify that which is capable of having a subjective experience.

provides evidence of something that is not part of the material universe as we understand it. And a prime example of this can be found within the nature and purpose of *questions* themselves. When examined closely, we see that questions are but expressions of a *yearning* to enhance our understanding—they are articulations of a *desire* to know more—and these are sentiments. The question posed by this chapter, then, becomes its own answer—the sentiment that provoked it can only exist as a product of something that is outside our understanding of the material universe. And because material qualities alone cannot account for all that is the human experience, we must therefore expand our criteria and continue probing beyond the limitations of the material world.

1.1

Qualities of the Material World	Qualities Not of the Material World
• Material characteristics (time, space, gravity, energy, particles, and so forth). • Neutral system, with all aspects locked into "indifference"; follows material laws alone, without exception (particles, regardless of arrangement or conditions, lack the ability to have preferences or objections). • No errors or fallacies, no such thing as imagination or delusions (in the history of the universe, no two particles ever bumped into each other the wrong way, or for the wrong reason).	• Life, awareness, consciousness, the ability to feel (includes the sense of value, wonder, curiosity, yearnings, and so forth). • Any position, view, or activity that can be characterized as a departure from the neutrality of matter and its characteristics. • Errors, fallacies, opinions, moral principles (specifically, the value we associate with them), products of the imagination (including false beliefs), and so forth.

In our attempts to understand reality, any characteristics (and their limitations) we identify must also apply to the arguments we make. And if the case is being made that all that exists is a material reality, then, to be consistent, the argument is restricted to using only those qualities that exist in a material world (left side of table) and nothing more—but this exercise cannot be completed within these limitations. The argument itself is an example of not being indifferent—it can only be made by reaching across the divide and borrowing from qualities that do not exist in a material reality (e.g., being curious about this question and acting on it, feeling it's important (or not), or even just stating that the opposing argument is wrong), but each time it does so, it violates its own premise.

EXPERIENCE

WHAT ELSE IS THERE?

With the development of more powerful telescopes and other observation equipment, scientists have been able to identify that there is not enough observable matter in galaxies for gravity to keep them together—by rights, galaxies should be torn apart but are not. Something, otherwise undetected, is generating enough gravity to keep galaxies rotating around their centers without the stars flying off into deep space. For lack of a better term, this "something" has come to be known as *dark matter*. Without taking it into account, any explanation of movement in the universe would be incomplete, if not incorrect. Scientists continue to study this phenomenon indirectly—because dark matter cannot be observed directly, they look for tell-tale signs that corroborate its existence. It thus becomes a case of finding and identifying the "fingerprints" that dark matter leaves behind.

Similarly, material characteristics cannot account for how atoms develop a sense of value or an ability to care, to feel, or to imagine anything, but we all experience these, and countless other sensations, on an ongoing basis. But even though a study of the material world will yield no clues as to how atoms are able to experience these sensations, it does not diminish the fact that these experiences are felt. Accordingly, any explanation of reality that does not take into account these qualities is, at best, incomplete. And because these sensations are felt, by necessity there must be "something" that is capable of experiencing them, with the question being, what is this something?

The something in question is the part of us that accounts for all the qualities inherent to a human being but which cannot be described strictly in material terms. This is the element that experiences life, that cares, that loves, that appreciates beauty, that is humbled by the mystery of life, and that can also suffer and be mistaken... it is our source of consciousness. This is what gives us sensitivity to the concepts of justice, and kindness, and honesty, and it is also the reason we have a sense of understanding,[2] which we then use to see that these qualities represent points in a wide spectrum and have opposites in injustice, and malice, and so forth.

Virtually all societies and cultures have references to this element, with the most common terms used to describe it being the soul, the spirit, the mind, or even just life. But these are just words, communication devices we employ to convey the meaning of something that falls outside our understanding of the material universe. Whatever objections there may be to these terms—whether because of religious, spiritual, or supernatural implications—they do not in any way take away from the fact that we experience and act on a sense of value. And because we cannot observe it directly, any attempts at understanding this source of consciousness (regardless of how you choose to refer to it) can also only be done indirectly. By focusing on those

---

[2] The sense of understanding that human beings display goes well beyond the mere ability to calculate. This is the reason why a chess computer needs to be able to calculate tens of thousands (in some cases even millions) of moves per second in order to defeat a human being who can only calculate moves at a rate that is probably in the low single digits per second. The reason is that human beings, to varying degrees, have the ability to understand the game and also a sense of intuition, which allows them to play the game of chess without having the raw calculation powers of a computer.

characteristics that are inherent to human beings but cannot be ascribed to matter, we can attempt to get a better understanding of this element and its significance.

But this is an undertaking that is fraught with complications, the least of which is not the problem of communication—we do not even so much as have a concise definition for the concept of "life" itself. Therefore, for the purposes of this work, the following definition for life will be used: *that which has the ability to feel.* No doubt this definition will prove inadequate, and many will not accept it because it cannot be quantified (a subjective experience cannot be registered by anything other than the entity experiencing it), but most of us recognize that this is the case— that living creatures can, and do, experience their environment on some level.

This definition is in sharp contrast to observations of the material world, which are limited to those things that can be measured and therefore are precise—observations and characteristics of what is felt or experienced cannot be measured, and therefore are exceedingly imprecise. We can calculate the age of the universe or the explosive force of a supernova, but we cannot measure the sense of awe we experience from these things. A thermometer will tell you how cold it is, but no instrument can tell how uncomfortable you are with the cold, much less how you feel watching a loved one suffer from the cold (it is worth noting here that what someone does in those circumstances can be regarded as a measure of character). Additionally, even though we cannot measure what is felt or in any way isolate what it is that has this ability, a chief marker of our humanity is how we treat those entities that we also perceive to have this ability to feel. Regardless, what is beyond contention is that we have the ability to feel. This ability, therefore, must make an appearance somewhere in our understanding of reality.[3]

Life is what makes it possible for us to experience whatever it is that we are experiencing, with any activity that can be construed as a departure from indifference falling exclusively under the purview of the living. But this ability to feel is no simple function: it is layered, complex, nuanced, and far-reaching—it touches everything. For example, we feel a certain way about what we experience through the five senses, social positions, and the outcome of our efforts; we also feel a certain way about knowledge and

---

[3] Not being able to quantify feelings or to identify what has the ability to experience them indicates a limitation to our abilities, not that these things do not exist.

information—and certainly about what to do with these. We not only are able to feel emotions but also feel a certain way about these same emotions and about being "too emotional"; we even feel a certain way about ourselves, our behavior, and so forth. We feel a certain way about feelings.

But because describing what we feel is highly subjective and because we use different language to communicate similar experiences, communicating these sensations has its inherent challenges (consider two individuals who both like a particular song attempting to describe why they like that song, and think also about how dissimilar the two descriptions are likely to be (and this, relatively speaking, represents a rather simple feeling or sensation—more complex feelings, such as the burning desire to feel successful on some level or the compulsion to adhere to certain principles, are significantly more challenging to communicate)). This lack of precision in communication, the ease with which our words can be misinterpreted, and the sense that something always gets lost when we attempt to put a feeling and its significance into words, all combine to make any attempts at communicating what we feel exponentially more challenging than communicating a measurement.

In addition to the ability to feel, we also have the ability to act on what we feel, with there being a vast, seemingly limitless, array of choices for our actions (which are the physical manifestations of breaking away from neutrality and indifference). Of all the different feelings that we are able to experience, we prefer—or value—some over others and therefore want to experience those sensations we value most while avoiding negative or unpleasant ones. In short, we feel that "A" is preferable to "B" and go with "A."

The process of expressing this sense of value begins with a feeling and then is followed by us using our mental faculties to explore the different options and considerations (including any possible counter feelings) before arriving at a particular position, and finally attempting to act in a manner that reflects that position. For example, an inner debate about having some ice cream might go something like this: We begin with the fact that we like ice cream and want to have some (wanting to experience the taste of ice cream is a feeling), but then consider that it's not necessarily the healthiest option, that it contributes to weight gain, or that maybe we are weak and lack resolve if we are unable to resist the desire to have some (we feel negatively about these considerations). Then we might consider that it's really okay to have a little bit once in a while, and so forth (thought process); finally, depending on how we answer our own internal questions and also how strongly we feel about any possible objections, we either end up having some or not (action).[4]

And here we can see why the action is an expression of value—in a general sense, the action represents the factor that perseveres over the other considerations in this process. There could be questions about whether our thought process was correct and led us to the right conclusion, but because the entire process at its core is a tug-of-war between feelings and counter feelings, it makes the resulting action an expression of value—even if only for a moment (we could eventually have second thoughts or regrets about our actions, and even feel they are not indicative

---

[4] To further illustrate the complexity of our ability to feel, here is a more detailed (yet far from comprehensive) attempt at a breakdown of this process: We feel the desire to have ice cream (this could be physical but may also be psychological); we feel (or experience) the taste of ice cream; we feel a certain way about the taste of ice cream (like it/don't like it); we feel a certain way about our actions themselves regarding ice cream (did we have some when we told ourselves we wouldn't?); we feel a certain way about ourselves regarding our actions in these circumstances (our ability to control our desire for ice cream—or anything really—can, and does, have an impact on how we feel about ourselves). And when put in a social context, it opens up a whole new world of possibilities and implications, and so forth.

of our values, but at that moment, in that set of circumstances, that particular feeling prevailed).

And when we take a closer look at this process, we see that the prevailing feeling itself is converted into an action—that the sense of value we experience acts like a force, taking what basically is a group of atoms and causing it to move in a specific manner (this is the point where the individual gets up and walks over to the fridge). And even though at our current level of understanding we cannot begin to fathom how a feeling can put a process in motion that leads to the movement of matter, this lack of understanding has never prevented anyone from using this ability in the course of living out their lives and doing whatever it is they feel they ought to be doing. But it must be emphasized that the feeling is what triggers the entire process— remove the feeling, and there is no process that leads to conscious actions, or expressions of value.

And this sense of value we experience doesn't just give direction to some of our actions but to *all* our conscious actions—it applies to the mundane as well as the profound. For instance, if we are passionate about a position or view, we will search for ways to immerse ourselves in developing our understanding of that position; if we want to have a certain lifestyle, we attempt to get an education and employment commensurate with that lifestyle; if we want to be good parents, we work to ensure that our children's emotional and material needs are met while preparing them for life as adults, and so forth. And at each of these undertakings we are met with challenges and difficulties that trigger counter feelings, but know we must find a way to work through these if we are to reach our goals. We basically derive a certain level of satisfaction, pleasure, validation, or a sense of fulfillment from certain courses of actions and their results, and act accordingly.

Life, in short, amounts to chasing a feeling, a sensation, or a sense of having done something valuable. If you think back upon your life, you will realize that any views, actions, positions, or accomplishments have all been the result of feeling one way or another about something—it is all a product of our ability to feel. And because this ability to feel and to express a sense of value is the driving element in life, not considering the source of this ability in our views and discussions of reality makes for a particularly glaring omission, one that profoundly impacts our understanding of the framework of reality.

But it does not stop there. The paradox of how an arrangement of atoms is able to have a subjective experience runs much deeper than mere questions about how we become aware of our physical environment—it goes beyond enjoying the taste of ice cream, the warm feeling of a touch, or anything that is experienced with the five senses. Even though there is no material explanation for how atoms are able to experience these sensations, this type of interaction has a direct material connection. But we are also able to experience a sense of love, empathy, compassion, justice, fulfillment, and other such qualities that have no direct material connection. And what is significant about these qualities is the deeper sense of value that we associate with them, which brings us to an additional quandary: is this deeper sense of value we experience real or an illusion? Do love and honesty actually have a deeper meaning, or are we just deceiving ourselves? If, indeed, we are speaking about illusions, we still need to account for the fact that *something* is experiencing these illusions, which brings us back again to some form of consciousness (after all, there is no explanation for how atoms/particles are able to experience illusions). The second part of the question, which addresses the intrinsic value of these qualities, will be discussed in greater detail in the following chapters.

Therefore, there is something that virtually all cultures since the dawn of humanity have made reference to that is the source of consciousness. This is what gives us the ability to feel and to experience reality and directs our actions through our sense of value—with the effects of this force on the aggregate total atoms in the human body being separate and distinct from the forces that prevail in the material universe. This is the reason why the taste of ice cream and other sundry pains and pleasures can exert such tremendous pressure on the activity of an arrangement of atoms; it is why this same arrangement of atoms can read poetry and find it haunting and beautiful, and why we frolic, bask in the glow of the setting sun, and lose ourselves in carefree laughter; it is also why a group of atoms can dedicate its efforts to pursuing a cause or ideal, even though causes and ideals have no meaning in a material universe. This conscious element cannot be measured or detected by material means. And because we are unable to observe directly what it actually is, we are limited to bringing our focus to what it does—and within a material universe where no aspect of it knows it exists, you are aware of yourself.

APOTHEOSIS

IS THERE A GOD?

B efore we tackle this question, we must clarify what we mean when we say "God." We all have heard expressions such as "he worships power" or "money is her god," which refer to those elements that individuals value the most. And because all of our actions and positions are expressions of value, when we take a position on an issue, we are expressing the value we hold for that position. And within our internal sense of values, we will hold some values higher than others—this is inescapable, otherwise we would not have the ability to disagree with anything. And the one element that we value above all others, that has the highest impact in our actions and goals, that motivates and inspires us above all else, is our own personal god.

Hence, when we say individuals have money or power as their god, we mean that their efforts are spent primarily on acquiring wealth, or power— even if at the expense of other principles—and go about their lives in a manner consistent with these goals. But these goals could be anything: they could be fame and material success, the accumulation of possessions or experiences, or the pursuit of pleasures and fulfillment of desires. They could even be the adherence to the principles of honesty, compassion, and so forth. Of the values we hold, by necessity, one must hold the highest place—therefore, we all have our personal gods.

But these gods (written with a lower case *g*) are not otherworldly entities possessing immense powers. They are just expressions of what we value most—representing the furthest point we have moved from indifference—and are real only in the context that they affect our actions. And then there is the view, espoused by the mono-theistic religions, of a supreme being that reigns atop all layers of reality. In some form or another, this is the view that most individuals hold of a God (with uppercase *G*), regardless of whether or not they personally believe in such an entity. Most religious and spiritual views have different descriptions of the characteristics of this God and also have different methods on how to relate to or worship this deity—with these differences usually being the cause of discord on this subject. This, in short, is the traditional view, which, by itself, does not prove or disprove the existence of God.

But there is another way of looking at this. As previously noted, in addition to the material world, there is something that is responsible for our ability to feel and for our sense of value, which is our source of consciousness. And our actions themselves are expressions of our inner sense of value. We can extrapolate from this that honesty/dishonesty, compassion/malice, love/hatred, etc. are all representations of this sense of value, albeit at opposite ends of the same spectrum. And our true positions in regards to these values are reflected primarily in our actions, not necessarily our words. (Think of an individual who claims to be a lover of justice but is unfair to those under his or her sphere of influence. In this case, is the sense of justice reflected in the words or actions?)

There could be several reasons why individuals' actions are not in harmony with their stated ideals: it could be due to willful misrepresentations, to a failure to fully grasp the meaning of the underlying concept, or the use of faulty logic could lead to incorrect conclusions. It could even be that the individual in the above example wanted to be a just person but succumbed to other pressures—that he faltered in his attempts to stay true to the principles of justice and allowed other, lesser sentiments to prevail (e.g., misrepresenting a situation in order to gain advantage). Regardless, actions represent an alternative language, one through which we more genuinely communicate our inner sense of value because words are more easily misapplied. In this sense, actions represent a truer language than words ever could.

Taking it further, these values are not absolutes but have degrees. For instance, it is easy to imagine different levels of injustice—history is littered with examples of wrongs being committed, with some being egregious (slavery, genocide), while others are insignificant in comparison (pocketing extra change that does not belong to you). And there is also a corresponding long history of individuals seeking justice and attempting to right wrongs, and sacrificing for the betterment of humanity. From here we can see that attempting to do positive things is in itself an expression of higher values, as opposed to supporting and engaging in unjust and hurtful courses of action.

Therefore, because our actions are driven by our sense of value and the conscious element is responsible for our actions, then our actions are representations of our inner level of values. Individuals are not honest because of their actions—they are honest because of their inner level of honesty, which is then projected on to their actions. And a quick glance of humanity reveals that individuals display different levels of these inner qualities as they navigate through life: some are more honest, while others are more caring, devoted, strong, understanding, and so forth. Actions are simple manifestations of the inner senses—they represent the values of the inner consciousness filtered through a material world.

It follows, then, that a person with a more developed level of honesty will display greater integrity in his or her affairs; a more compassionate individual will be more caring; a stronger one will be more capable of resisting the appeal of lower sentiments and will strive to be more than just a product of his or her environment, and so forth. The model that we are working with here is that there are different levels of development of these inner values, which in turn correspond to the level of consciousness. This means that actions, or expressions of value, are indicators of the inner level of consciousness—with more developed levels of consciousness displaying a higher level of values.

Using this as a base, we can envision a progression of higher levels of consciousness, rising to an increasingly more perfect state, more evolved and purer in its objectives, extending well beyond our ability to understand. Bearing in mind the complexities of the human experience and the vastness of the universe, with untold expanses and mysteries, consider a level of consciousness that is perfect in its expression of love, peace, and compassion, that is complete in every way, without the wisp of a blemish, infinitely beyond the appeal of lower sentiments—with this being a level of consciousness that is above all mysteries, material and otherwise, which from our lowly positions can only be regarded as master of the universe—is this God?

Once we have established that there are different levels of consciousness, then by necessity there must be a highest level. And unless we are prepared to make the case that we represent the highest point ourselves, then we must accept that there is something higher. The question then becomes, what do we call this apotheosis of consciousness? Terms such as the "Universal," the "Divine," the "Source," the "Almighty," the "Creator," or "Nirvana," along with many other religious appellations, have been used in attempts to describe this level of consciousness and its characteristics. But any terms we use are also just words—mere semantics—conveying our vision of something that is far beyond our ability to understand. Of much greater significance are the characteristics of this level of consciousness, and what they mean to us.

But here we venture into terrain that is beyond our abilities, and we run into the problem of describing characteristics of the ability to feel, in the grandest of all scales. We can frame our descriptions of the highest level of consciousness in the context of a benign, powerful force, using terms such as "the perfect expression of love," but we are still relying on a definition to convey an ability to love and to express values at a level that exceeds ours by a factor so great that no sense of proportion can be established between the two that makes any sense. And because understanding is a characteristic of consciousness, it follows that a higher level of consciousness, by definition, will have a level of understanding that exceeds ours, placing it outside the boundaries of our own limitations. In other words, understanding it is simply beyond us.

What we can do, however, is identify some

qualities that are not applicable in this context. First, because something perfect has no needs as we understand them, any activity we consider necessary in order to relate to this level of consciousness (such as worship or adoration) addresses *our* needs only. We should also not make the mistake of thinking we have no needs or shortcomings, which can result in our projection of these same shortcomings onto our descriptions of the highest level of consciousness, which in turn impacts our understanding of it. Therefore, any description that is gender specific, includes negative qualities (such as anger, jealousy, vindictiveness, or the desire to punish), displays self-serving tendencies, is unable to forgive, is offended by the name or label we use when referring to it, dictates final outcomes based on arbitrary circumstances, or relies on fear as a tool, among other examples of the human qualities and shortcomings we project on to it, cannot be regarded as an accurate description of the highest level of consciousness but rather, of something smaller.[5]

---

[5] For the purpose of this work, unless otherwise specified, the term God is used as a reference to the highest level of consciousness and not in a traditionally religious context.

Permanence

Is Death the End?

There are only two possible answers to this question: either death is an end—total oblivion, a change to absolute indifference, a complete cessation of consciousness forevermore—or it is a separation, where a level of consciousness commonly referred to as an immortal soul survives physical death in a nonmaterial world (which we will refer to as an *expanded reality*). These are the two bases, creating differing frameworks for reality, with each one functioning under a different set of rules. Because we cannot observe directly whether or not death is the end, reality and our sense of value must be understood and explained either in the context that it all ends at death or that life continues somehow. And in this latter point, because life is not material in nature, the focus must not be on any material aspects but on the surviving element's qualities—with these being primarily the ability to feel and to experience a sense of value. Do these continue?[6]

In order to explore this question, we will begin by looking at the question of the significance of values that was raised in chapter II. As previously indicated, no known process describes how we are able to experience a sense of value, but at this part of the argument we are moving our focus to the other side of the question of values. Meaning, we are no longer looking at how values are experienced but rather, at what they actually mean: do the values we experience have actual intrinsic value, or are they mere illusions? In other words, why is "good" good, and "bad" bad? We must keep in mind that we are not settling for a "that's just the way it is" type of answer and therefore must press further.

---

[6] Because the ability to feel exists, and because it cannot be linked to matter—to the atoms that make up the human body—the question about death really is a question about whether this ability to feel ceases (changes) at physical death or not. Therefore, the common argument for death being the end because of a lack of empirical evidence supporting the concept that life continues, presupposes that the ability to feel ceases at physical death. But because there is an equal lack of empirical evidence to support that it ceases or continues, this line of argument leads to a logical dead end.

When we consider the nature of values, we realize that for anything to have value, it must be based on something—always. When you think of the dollar, it has value because of the power of the US Treasury. Remove the backing of this institution, and the dollar becomes like Monopoly money—it loses its value. Accordingly, when we decide that qualities such as honesty and integrity are positive, we are recognizing their value. The question then becomes, what is this value based on? And the answer to this question can be characterized in one of two ways: either the sense of value we experience is based on personal preferences (these are subjective values, which means that an opposing view of honesty has equal value), or it is based on something else (this would be something that has value independently of our personal preferences). And this is the key to the argument—the basis for our values, and whether their significance lies solely on our ability to have preferences and act on them, or if they in fact have a higher, objective basis. In other words, we may have the ability to choose A over B and to act on it, but is there a set of circumstances where A actually is a more meaningful option than B?

And when we take a closer look at this question, the first point that can be established is that if we are locked in an existence where nothing is experienced beyond physical death—meaning there is no other side, no expanded reality, nothing "behind the veil," so to speak—then whether we like it or not, the values we experience have no basis other than our ability to experience them and therefore can only be subjective—not some, but *all* values are subjective (regardless of how we came to experience them). The reason is because in a "death is the end" premise, by definition, the end result is always the same, regardless of choices made or values upheld. The just and the tyrant, the kind and the cruel, the hard worker and the slacker, the principled and the corrupt, the faithful and the skeptical, the celebrated and the obscure—they are all, without exception, assured the exact same fate. (Consider that if death is the end, then from the perspective of someone who has lived and died, the fact that he or she actually lived becomes utterly without meaning—much less the type of life that was lived.)

Because in this premise choices and values have no impact whatsoever on the outcome of life—because they fall under the "ultimately it does not matter" category, it means they have no value beyond our ability to experience them (and only while we still have the ability to experience them), and this means they are subjective. In this context, the answer to the question, "Do some values have greater meaning than others?" is always no. There simply is no way around this point, leaving us to contend with the implications of such a view of reality—but these are not, by any means, minor implications. And because this premise limits our experience to subjective values only, then the next logical step is to see how this limitation holds up when applied to life in general.

Subjective values, by definition, only have significance to the individual experiencing them, which means they do not rise to the level of being debatable (unless it is done for sport). When analyzed closely, we see that subjective values aren't values at all in the context that we understand values to be; they are mere preferences, inclinations, tendencies, likes, and dislikes. We may "value" them personally, and even though our words and actions are expressions of these values, that's as far as their significance goes—they are completely disconnected from any question of greater meaning. These values represent just another sensation we experience— a different flavor of ice cream—with personal satisfaction often being the primary goal.

It must be emphasized that the view of a

reality restricted to subjective values does not eliminate the sense of right and wrong or even diminish our ability to experience it. The question really is not about experiencing a sense of right and wrong, because we clearly do. The question is whether this sense of right and wrong has any value beyond our ability to experience it, and within this point of view, it simply does not—but this creates an impossible problem: if the sense of right and wrong is stripped of all intrinsic value, if for all effective purposes it is neutralized, with there being no set of circumstances where it has meaning, then we become powerless to disagree with anything, including this argument, in a meaningful way.

The reality is that in a world of subjective values, the only valid consideration in making one choice over another, no matter how noble or depraved the intentions, is what the individual making the choice feels or wants to experience. In this world, whatever causes we champion, whatever good we try to do, or even whatever suffering we may cause, are all at best mere illusions. Whatever sense of value (positive or negative) we attach to these courses of action is hollow—it is all for naught, with oblivion being the only certainty. Within this context, trying to make the case that one position is better than another, even if the argument is so well conceived as to reveal a touch of genius, is akin to trying to determine whether certain notes of Monopoly money have more value than others: they do, but they really don't. Absent a grounding factor, values become arbitrary.

It follows that within this setting, anyone who stops to reflect on what is the right thing to do, considers which worldview is more accurate, struggles with his or her conscience in moments of doubt, or searches for some greater meaning, does so in vain—to consider the significance of our actions beyond personal implications is an empty gesture. Here, and from their inner perspectives, the actions of a Mother Teresa or of a Jack the Ripper (feel free to substitute for any names you like) have no meaning beyond satisfying whatever wants or desires these individuals sought to experience during their life-times. And as those who have delved deeply into these questions have noted, this produces a view that reduces life to an existence without purpose, with individuals going about their meaningless routines, engaging in repetitive, empty actions, blind to the absurdity of it all.

But when we take this premise and examine its practical applications closely, a very telling point becomes apparent: the subjectivization of values, even though great fodder for philo-sophical discussions, can only exist in the world of words and ideas—in polite conversations or the clinical sterility of books—and not in real-life circumstances, which can be ugly and brutal. When this premise is exposed to the "reality on the ground," its significance completely vanishes. In the language of actions, which trumps our articulated positions, this view is categorically rejected by virtually all of humanity. To illus-trate this point, think of circumstances where an individual is subjected to an unprovoked cruel assault. If values were truly subjective, it would mean that the assailant's desire to assault and commit mayhem is equal in value to the victim's desire not to be assaulted—and what this really would mean is that brute force (or any expression of a base desire) is as valid a deciding factor as any questions of right or wrong. But this, again, is a premise that is rejected by all—even the assailant would reject this premise if the tables were turned and he became the victim.

And this active rejection of the subjectiviza-tion of values does not apply to just physically harmful or injurious circumstances—it also applies to any type of relationship or interaction that is fundamentally exploitative or unfair, is based on deceit, or causes some level of distress, among other considerations. These types of interactions are inherently understood to be negative in nature, a fact that is reflected in our use of language (individuals who engage in such behavior are referred to as dishonest, insincere, abusive, self-serving, and so forth).

This principle has the power to mold societies. It forms the foundation for our social institutions, including a judicial system we consider to be "good" or "advanced" (with laws against dishonest and harmful behavior being applied equally to all). Keeping in mind that prehistoric men and women did not have a legal code, we can see that the creation of an early set of rules or laws was a direct result of identifying behavior that was deemed to be wrong or undesirable on some level.

And as humanity has progressed, our legal system continues to evolve around this sense of justice (which is just a code word for a facet of our sense of right and wrong), with a good judicial system being the union of what is *right* and what is legal. Because justice is something that is felt, the legal code we create represents the imperfect art of taking this sense of justice and attempting to craft a set of rules, or laws, that somehow embody it and also reflect the objective nature of this principle. Otherwise there would

49

be no bad laws (the legal standard would simply be the standard of what is right), but history and common sense tell us differently. Events and circumstances are not "bad" or "wrong" because there are laws against them—we recognize, sometimes through lengthy and painful ordeals (e.g., slavery) that they represent a negative and then adjust our legal system accordingly. And because this is a recurring pattern in history, we can therefore see that the forward march of humanity is based on the active opposition to the subjectivization of values, and that this stance, which supersedes our articulated positions, is a major component for our outlook in life—it cannot be separated from our ability to function, either privately or collectively.

Because the view of a reality restricted to subjective values can only exist in the abstract and not in real-life circumstances, we must therefore consider the question of what happens at death and examine the other possible outcome. Here, the argument must be consistent with the concept that a level of consciousness survives physical death. Within this setting, our actions stand for something—they become as "currency" that has value in an expanded reality. And when we look closely at this view, we find that it is a staple of humanity—not necessarily that values are followed consistently, but they are recognized as having greater significance than mere preferences. Ultimately, and even though there is considerable disagreement on what constitutes right and wrong behavior, humanity acknowledges that the sense of right and wrong is not illusory. (Logically, can anyone say this is wrong?) This means that the answer to the question, "Do some values have greater significance than others?" is yes—that the final outcome is not always the same, that choices made, or values upheld, have meaning on a greater level—that A, in some cases, does indeed have a greater meaning than B.

To explore this point, we can start by looking at the one value that virtually all individuals agree on: that it is wrong for them as individuals to be taken advantage of or be treated badly or unfairly. This is because, to put it in very simple terms, when we are treated badly, we experience a level of distress, and we don't want to experience negative feelings. And what gives us a shared sense of humanity is the recognition that others, like ourselves, also want to experience the opposite of distress.

Accordingly, the progression of humanity throughout the ages has been one of taking this principle and applying it to ever larger circles of humanity—meaning that not only are individuals we identify with our equals on the human scale, but *all* are. This includes and applies to all men and women regardless of racial, cultural, religious, social, and economic backgrounds—it is symbolic of the recognition that the conscious element present within all of us is what gives us our human worth—with this principle being at the heart of the universal dictum, "Do unto others as you would have done unto yourselves."

And the value of this principle cannot be overemphasized. Consider that the great crimes against humanity—the episodes of genocide, the inhumane bondage, the crushing displays of oppression, along with other acts of horrifying cruelty—at their core represent an abrogation of this principle. When these occurrences are examined closely, we see that they can take place only when a group views itself as superior (whether from racial, cultural, intellectual, economic, gender, or religious differences, and so forth) and deserving of a higher position, and views the lives of a second group as not having quite the same value—if any value at all.

It is this failure to see the same level of humanity in others that we see in ourselves, especially when it reaches a cultural level or we allow it to become institutionalized, that creates circumstances where great injustices can become justified. Therefore, if we are serious in our efforts to prevent the repetition of these blights against humanity, then this is where we must place our sentinels: we must guard against any indication that another's humanity is diminished and must also accept the bitter truth that this is not a "them" affliction—it is an "us" affliction—and as such, this vigil must always begin with our own selves.

And if we are to also consider the opposite side of this point, we will recognize that individuals who selflessly dedicate their lives to the betterment of humanity, who work towards increasing understanding, fight against oppressive measures, sacrifice in order to decrease conditions that cause suffering, and so forth (all efforts which can be filed under the "labor of love" category), are consistently regarded among the better examples of humanity. This is a constant, regardless of religious, spiritual, or secular views of reality (excluding the most radical and fanatical voices from these camps). And the position shared by a great majority of humanity—indeed the very language that humanity speaks—is that the sense of value behind these actions and views has a higher, objective value.

In conclusion, it follows logically that the view that death is the end equates to a position where a material reality eventually prevails—but adherence to this position also means acceptance of *all* the limitations within this premise. But this position has as a setting a universe that is filled with "stuff" that cannot care and is governed by laws that are as indifferent as they are pervasive, creating an impossible problem. And the problem isn't that this position sidesteps the question of what is it that actually experiences values, or even that it writes off the ability of a bunch of atoms "sharing an experience" as unexplained physical phenomena. The problem is that this position takes the sense of value we experience and renders it completely meaningless, leaving us with a setting that reduces reality to a mere arrangement of atoms and particles, with different situations and circumstances being but different arrangements of these units of matter—with not one set of circumstances, no matter how sublime or horrifying, being better or worse than any other, regardless of whatever meaningless feelings we may have about them.

This setting takes everything we hold dear and rips the significance out. In this world, because higher values are illusory, we don't have the luxury of selecting a few and holding on to them—neither the ones we really like nor any needed for society to function—they all must be surrendered. This is a world where we may have the ability to choose A over B, but ultimately no one option has greater significance than another; where we become powerless to make a valid point or raise objections to a view we disagree with, because to do so is to assign a lesser value to the counterpoint; where any attempts at increasing our understanding become meaningless (they represent the ideal that being in a state of "knowing" and "understanding" is better than not, but this is just another variation of A being better than B); where what we call "moral" or "ethical" behavior cannot be grounded in anything other than empty preferences; where we cannot even substantiate that "evil" is actually a negative (beyond what is experienced by the victims). This ultimately has the effect of taking all our personal positions and efforts and reducing them to mere "sporting endeavors"—because in the end nothing matters, with the end result always being a return to absolute indifference, it all becomes an exercise in futility—but therein lies the fatal flaw: to take the view that death is the end and to present it as a position worth knowing is to invoke an expanded reality.

And at some stage we need to recognize these efforts for what they are—and they are but attempts at making the point that ours is a pointless existence. If it is all an illusion, then the value of knowing this is an illusion too. Therefore, and regardless of how strongly some of us may feel about this position, this ceases to be a functioning premise once all aspects of reality are plugged in.

By comparison, a setting where a level of consciousness survives physical death is the only possible alternative in which higher values are not illusory. Within this expanded reality there are positive and negative values, and in our attempts to identify and express these values, we use terms such as love, peace, compassion, justice, kindness, courage, altruism, increased understanding, and so forth for the positives, and injustice, cruelty, malice, dishonesty, greed, selfishness, willful ignorance, and others for the negatives. It is also telling that although the value of the positive qualities is sometimes brought into question (and can even be dismissed as nothing more than inane, maudlin expressions of sentimentality), the negative qualities are never dismissed (no one regards malice and cruelty as illusions, especially when directed at themselves). But these qualities represent opposite ends of the same spectrum—and in order to function within the confines of logical thought, we must either acknowledge or disavow the significance of both sides equally.

In the end, the best indicators for the significance of the values we experience can be found by looking at humanity as a whole and seeing within its tumultuous history ongoing attempts to carve a more meaningful existence than one of just acting out base desires and also to elevate civilization to a plane ever higher than that of mere brutes. The answer lies in the recognition that these efforts themselves represent something with a deep, vibrant, positive value—the very meaning of being a civilized species rests on this. Ultimately, and regardless of how we articulate this point, this means that in our most genuine mode of expressing values—the language of actions—the view that death is not the end is a driving force in humanity.

PURPOSE

WHY ARE WE HERE?

This might be the biggest question of all. Not to diminish the significance of other questions, but when it's all said and done, it comes down to, "What does this mean for me?" This is the "What's it all about?" question, and it strikes at the heart of what gives life meaning. And any attempts at understanding this question and any possible conclusions require that we take into consideration an account of reality that is as complete as possible. The previous chapters, which led to the premise that the conscious element retains certain characteristics once disconnected from the material, were an attempt to cover the terrain necessary to arrive at this question. Therefore, the question at this point can only be made from within this context—it must ask: *for what purpose would an immortal entity be connected to a mortal body?*

We can start by focusing on our ability to feel, which (as has been previously noted) encompasses a wide range of what the conscious element is able to experience. Within this range, what we experience on an everyday basis can be broken down into two categories: it can be from either an external or internal source, with each type of experience affecting us in a different way.

External feelings are derived from our circumstances and have worldly connections. This begins with what we experience from the five senses but also includes such diverse sensations as what we experience from praise, pleasures, social status, wealth, fame, power, glory, or success (and their corresponding opposites), and so forth. These experiences, along with our genetic makeup, environment, conditioning, ability to reason, and other circumstances not only affect how we feel but also create an image or persona with which we strongly identify (a psychological profile where we use expressions such as "the self" or "the ego" in our attempts to identify and describe this characteristic) but which ultimately has an external basis. Because we can develop deep attachments to these external sensations and also because we are essentially looking to experience certain feelings, they all apply considerable pressure to the choices we make—but they are still our choices to make.

Inner feelings are subtler—they are more difficult to express and harder still to justify, but they can be most powerful. They are what the conscious element experiences within and about itself (linked to our conscience). These inner feelings can be profoundly unsettling or deeply satisfying—they represent the inner sense that warns us that we could be veering off path, that our efforts are not on par with our abilities, or that there is value in certain undertakings. They are the reason we have a sense of right and wrong and why we feel strongly there are certain things we should do or avoid doing.

The contrast between these two types of sensations is that one is based primarily on the tangibles—on what the experience or the results themselves feel like—while the other runs deeper and gives us a sense of whether or not we should engage in such behavior. And this distinction can create circumstances where we act in a manner that produces positive external feelings but causes us to feel otherwise internally (or vice versa). For example, if we freely indulge our appetites, or betray a trust, or give in to our urges and engage in reckless behavior that may affect others negatively, or if we steal glory by cheating someone out of recognition they justly earned, and so forth, we might experience positive external sensations (e.g., pleasurable, delicious, profitable, and so forth), but this type of behavior might lead to an inner level of dissatisfaction, such as a sense of regret, or of letting others down. Eventually this sense of dissatisfaction could reach the point where it prompts changes in our behavior, where we seek out a manner of acting that is more consistent with positive inner feelings.

Conversely, the opposite approach has a different effect: if we demonstrate courage, behave in an honorable manner, or take a stand on principle and advance a worthwhile cause, one that benefits others, even if it comes at significant personal cost (which could cause negative external sensations, such as some form of hardship or sacrifice), it could cause us to feel that we have accomplished something that has positive value—we will feel good about it internally. Think of individuals who identify a need in society—a social injustice somewhere, for example—and dedicate their efforts to changing these circumstances, foregoing more profitable options and accepting a more challenging course in life. In this example, it seems right that they should be recognized for their efforts, but there is a deeper sense of fulfillment that is experienced even if the actions are not recognized.

Another significant factor to consider when contrasting these two types of sensations is the timeframes involved. The gratification from external feelings is usually much faster and can even be immediate (there is no delay in experiencing the sensations from our five senses). And even though some aspects of external sensations can take longer to come to fruition, in a general sense, they are characterized by quicker results. Inner feelings, however, take longer and cannot be rushed—they need time for us to take in and process the significance of what we have done, and of the manner in which we have led our lives—in certain instances requiring a lifetime (or beyond) before we can fully understand their significance.

Because the ability to feel is central to both types of sensations, the significance of this ability is all-encompassing: to an entity that has this ability, the only thing that matters is what is felt; to anything else, nothing matters (think of a brick, and of what could possibly matter to it). This means that any experience, from within the entirety of all possible experiences, no matter how significant or trivial, can only affect you in one of two ways: either how you feel about it, or how you feel about and within yourself, in regards to your actions in those circumstances. There is nothing in the realm of what we can experience that is outside these two possibilities—from an inner perspective, this represents all there is.

Of these two types of sensations, the internally based ones are superior (e.g., honesty before profit) because they go to our very cores and are not dependent on external stimuli. The individual whose actions are based primarily on inner values exhibits a greater sense of purpose and control. Compare this to an individual who is motivated primarily by external stimuli, who is, in effect, at the mercy of external circumstances (think of someone who does something because it is the right thing to do, as opposed to someone who does something expecting praise or reward). And as we continue exploring this premise, we inevitably arrive at the realization that an over-abundance of positive external sensations can still leave us feeling empty inside.

We must therefore focus on the inner feelings that we are able to experience, which themselves can range from negative to positive. We use expressions such as distress, unrest, regret, sadness, shame, despair, and a sense of failure or unfulfilled potential to characterize the feelings on one end of the spectrum, and serenity, wholeness, peace, happiness, and fulfillment on the other. But these are mere words used to convey the range of what we can experience. Within this range we can envision the highest level of consciousness as being complete in every way, having overcome all possible obstacles to reach this level, experiencing a sense of absolute fulfillment, and being in a state of perfect harmony and understanding—with this being the level of consciousness that experiences the greatest inner experience that can be experienced. It follows logically, then, that what we want to accomplish more than anything else, or our overarching objective in this earthly life, is to have our own inner experience approach this exalted level—we want to increase our inner feelings of fulfillment and wellness and decrease any sense of distress or incompleteness we may have: we want to rise. The question is—how is this achieved?

Our lives on this Earth, with the countless obstacles and innumerable choices we have, present us with opportunities to grow in so many ways. By using our ability to reason and by developing an understanding of ourselves and our circumstances, we are better able to cultivate qualities in our person and also give direction to our actions in ways consistent with our inner desire for growth. For instance, to fight for justice is to rise on the plane of justice; to guard against harming others and resist taking advantage of the vulnerable is to become stronger; to act in a selfless manner, using our abilities to benefit others, is to recognize the human value inherent in all—a critical element for growth. To so much as engage in a simple act of compassion is to approach God.

This is what gives meaning to our deepest sense of value. Actions that are consistent with the overall objective of increasing our inner sense of fulfillment and wellness have the greatest value (or are what we call "good"), while negative actions or harmful behaviors are not. That is why justice, honesty, compassion, and the like are positives—engaging these principles is consistent with us moving closer to our objective, while their respective opposites represent a derailment of our efforts or of us succumbing to lower sentiments and "losing our way."

Basically, a course of action that impacts others positively is "good." And if this good in question impacts external feelings only, then it is a smaller good (it could even have a counter effect, as in making things too easy for someone else may abate their hunger for growth)—whereas cultivating views and circumstances that encourage and promote behavior consistent with positive inner feelings is a greater good.[7] It is important to note that the overall objective we seek is never in conflict with the objectives of others. On the contrary, helping others move forward is one of the pillars for inner growth. (Compare this to external sensations, such as our desires, ambitions, and appetites, which very often are at odds with the best interests of others, and if not kept in check, could easily encroach on their well-being and dignity.)

A natural outgrowth of this view, where we are seeking to enhance our inner experience and the objective is to reach a higher level, is that obstacles and challenges we face in life are hurdles, with each obstacle that is overcome being symbolic of us becoming bigger than that obstacle. Keeping in mind that "the harder the battle, the sweeter the victory," when we therefore take this premise and distill it to its essence, we see that the challenges we face in life are not mere obstacles that keep us from enjoying a more pleasant existence—they are the engines

---

[7] We are not able to affect inner feelings of others directly, but we are, to an extent, able to create and influence circumstances that encourage and inspire the types of behavior that are conducive to positive inner feelings.

that drive our inner growth. This is the reason why perseverance in the face of the most difficult and challenging scenarios—of knowing we were not bested by external circumstances, no matter how severe—is a source of inner satisfaction. This is what gives rise to the inner sense of "I fought my battles, and within my abilities and circumstances, did the best I could"—which is a particularly powerful and fulfilling inner sensation.

Ultimately, inner feelings are the result of how we have led our lives and how genuine our efforts have been—and if these actions are grounded in higher values, then the greater the positive inner impact, even if this is not clear at the time of the action. Having a mental perspective that is consistent with this premise—where there is a purpose to it all—helps us to better prepare ourselves and to cultivate qualities consistent with this objective, regardless of external circumstances.

It must be noted that this premise differs from a punishment/reward model that is the mainstay of many religious views. By examining it closely, we see that a punishment/reward premise does not fare well logically. Briefly, such a premise calls for a higher being (God) to place lower beings (us) in circumstances that are either distressing or pleasant (punishment/reward), with how we have approached this entity (worshipped) and also dealt with others being a significant factor in determining the punishment/reward outcome. Admittedly this is an oversimplified synopsis, but it does represent some of the basics as understood by most individuals. The problem here is that with the possible exception of how we have interacted with others, this model is based on and functions primarily at the level of external sensations, which are inferior to inner sensations—and this is inconsistent with any understanding we can have of the highest level of consciousness and of our approach to it.

A more logical scenario has as a base our desire to grow, to rise to a higher level of consciousness and experience a greater sense of inner well-being, and it takes into account that *understanding* is a prerequisite for growth. As our understanding increases, at some point we will have intimate understanding of the effects of all our actions—it stands to reason that if we acted primarily in a self-serving manner, taking advantage of others, or caused pain and suffering, proper understanding of these actions and their effects will be at least as distressing as the effects of our actions. In short, negative actions we engage in result in negative external feelings for others, but will eventually be the source of negative inner feelings for ourselves. This will in turn add to our inner level of distress, fueling the desire for an opportunity to correct this wrong—all of which is consistent with our inner desire for growth.

"All the world is a stage" says the bard, and we "merely players." The roles we play on this Earth are those of imperfect entities seeking some level of improvement, yearning to experience a higher sense of fulfillment, wanting to overcome those limitations that prevent us from moving to a higher level. And Earth is the arena that provides opportunities for such growth. It is a setting where the qualities of the conscious element are assaulted by the demands of the self and where the resulting entanglements expose our weaknesses and compel us to confront our shortcomings. It is a battleground where inner feelings are pitted against external feelings, where we strive to find the proper balance between these two epic forces, with one benefitting primarily the self and producing results that are temporal and quickly dissipate, whereas the results of the other go to our very cores—and those results we do take with us.[8]

---

[8] External feelings need a material medium in order to be experienced and therefore have significance in a material, worldly realm. Once

This earthly existence is but a field of challenges that pushes us to the limits of our understanding and endurance. The obstacles we face, the hardships we encounter, the travails that are a constant in our lives—external sensations all—are fleeting in nature, mere blips against the backdrop of the infinite. Each individual, in his or her own way, by facing their unique challenges and by addressing individual needs and circumstances, slowly inches forward towards a common goal.

By taking the qualities we associate with the highest level of consciousness and incorporating them into our actions—that is, by actively adhering to the principles of love, peace, and

---

disconnected from the material, the conscious element (it follows logically) functions primarily with inner feelings. This means that from an inner perspective, physical death also means a cessation of the existence of the self, and, by extension, those qualities and characteristics associated with it also cease to have significance.

In addition, to give some clarification on what is meant by the self, think of a puppet, which is just inanimate matter. But when it is controlled by a puppeteer, it generates a certain image, such as being funny, or clever, or silly—but it's really none of those things; it's just matter—with the image, which corresponds to the self, existing only in our imagination. And if the puppet itself had the ability to feel and to act on those feelings, then it would also feel a certain way about this image, which would then be reflected in its actions. Consequently, behavior that prioritizes this image, or the self, can be characterized as being "self-serving," or "ego-driven," as opposed to actions based on principle.

compassion and by reaching deep within to find the strength to not allow inner feelings to be compromised for the sake of external ones, we grow. And the gains we experience from living out these principles are *not* fleeting in nature—these actions transform the conscious element into an entity of higher consciousness—and thus enhance the universe.

It follows then, that the *modus operandi* that is most consistent with our highest purpose in this life, to put it simply, is to have God as our god; that life is to be embraced with all its gifts; that we are enriched immeasurably by bringing more than we take; that recognizing and respecting the humanity of all those who cross our path (regardless of external factors) is a display of strength; that we live in the face of sublime greatness and should not walk in fear and trepidation, but should face our obstacles with bold determination and a measure of humility; and that, above all, the greatest of all meanings is to be found in exiting the arena… a little bigger than we entered it.[9]

---

[9] If you think about the eulogies that are given upon the death of an individual, by their very nature they represent those qualities that our deepest understanding recognizes as having greatest value when considering the significance of a life that has been lived. And these tributes normally gravitate towards examples of how the individual

may have had a positive impact on family, friends, and/or society—and also of being true to their own person, while adhering to valuable principles, overcoming obstacles and hardships, achieving certain goals, inspiring others to reach higher, and so forth—all of which are consistent with the underlying, if unstated, principles of spiritual growth and advancement. In other words, they represent examples of getting closer to God.

FINAL THOUGHTS

The great religions are vehicles that, at their core, serve the purpose of inspiring humanity to act in a manner consistent with getting closer to God. They are anchors to a values-based system (which is nonexistent in a material universe). But these institutions, which are thousands of years old, reflect the views of their time and speak a language that is increasingly out of harmony with the demands of modern understanding. They have been, over the centuries, under the stewardship of flawed men (as all men and women are), with some being considerably less than noble individuals, resulting in severe missteps. This has created a distorted sense of value where the worldly characteristics of these religions (e.g., the name attributed to God, membership in a specific religion or denomination, the rituals and dogmas, the location of worship, and other material aspects) often are held forth as what has true value, while the principles of love, peace, and compassion are relegated to lesser positions. This has resulted in a decrease in the sense of legitimacy that is felt behind some of their messages, which is our inner sense of value telling us that this does not feel quite right. And the insistence, in some cases, of holding on to a material view of the universe that is outdated and (in plain English) wrong, has made these institutions easy targets and opened them up to considerable ridicule.

But many of the voices that most loudly decry these institutions and what they represent are not presenting an alternative view that inspires humanity to do better. This has created a vacuum, leading to aimlessness and confusion, and the acrimonious tone of the debate has led many to distance themselves from these questions. But a theme of this work is that the realm of consciousness is a voluntary, not coercive, system, where we alone are responsible for our actions and their consequences. Accordingly, our mere presence on this Earth—on this field of obstacles—is indicative of our desire to take the opportunities found herein and use them as catalysts for growth. And considering that squandered opportunities are often among our deepest regrets, it follows that just coasting along is not the option that will yield the most desirable results.

To better understand our roles, consider the steps necessary to become a physician. It begins with a vision—with a goal to attain, followed by an effort to understand what this quest entails—of its significance for ourselves and for those we will touch. And then comes the work—lots, and lots, and lots of work—and then, more work. Long nights, being pushed to the limit, being required to master all areas needed for this field, questioning if it's worth it, and wondering when it will be over. It's a process that takes strength, dedication, and commitment and that calls for a sense of sacrifice and for the wherewithal to resist the distractions and temptations that could derail these efforts. And at long last, when this process is complete, the results, accompanied by a profound sense of accomplishment, arrive in the form of a piece of paper confirming the status of doctor. But the diploma is not a reward; it is not what makes a doctor, a doctor—this position is earned. The efforts themselves that went into attaining this goal are transformative. This whole process takes a non-doctor and gradually transforms the individual into a doctor—the diploma is mere recognition and celebration of a successful transformation (the real meaning lies in being able to function at this level).

In the same manner, we are all on a journey of untold significance, where living according to the highest principles has a transformative effect, and reaching a higher level of consciousness is not a reward—it is earned. This process also takes strength, vision, understanding, and effort... an immense amount of effort. Each individual is responsible for his or her efforts, but if the goals are unclear or if the understanding is somehow lacking, then it could create circumstances where the efforts being exerted are not in line with our highest objective.

Ultimately, the goal is not to have any goals but to be perfect expressions of love, compassion, and other qualities that transcend the human experience, but if I may be allowed a personal view here, we still have some ways to go yet. Humanity, in a general sense, seems to be at a level of spiritual development where the self still represents a daunting challenge—where we are still susceptible to the appeal of lower sentiments, where we can still be seduced away from higher objectives by the lure of worldly gratifications, where we can still be prevented from facing our challenges by faltering courage and wavering resolve, where we can still be confounded and have our efforts sabotaged by flawed reasoning and misguided ideals, and where our actions too often still betray a less-then-developed sense of justice. This is what makes taking on the self, or living life, a quest like no other—it puts us in a realm that is both beautiful and tragic, uplifting and exacting, full of promise and yet unforgiving. But this is also a setting where we can reap immeasurable benefits by facing these very challenges (we overcome them by taking them on), where the principles of love, peace, and compassion are the beacons that will never betray us, and where a selfless approach to our efforts, which requires so much inner fortitude to sustain, is a particularly powerful tool available to us.

But in the midst of it all, we still need road-maps and other aides to help us overcome the shortcomings of our less-than-perfect level of understanding and to provide a general direction for our efforts. This is the impetus behind this work—it dates back to a personal quest to better understand our world and our function in it. I share it here in the hopes that reasoning through these questions can help bring our highest objective into focus, and that this could be a useful addition to the understanding portion of the process. The conclusions were not arrived at lightly—they draw from all fields, ancient and modern, and every effort has been made to ensure that they are consistent with a modern view of the material universe. There is much that remains outside our circle of understanding, but that in no way should be an obstacle in continuing to work towards the goal whose significance stands above all others.

I thank you for your time... may the path you choose lead to an ever-greater sense of fulfillment.